Introduction

This book is a selection of some of the things I have written, poems, ditties, songs and sketches, paintings and drawings (to include the cover) I have done between 1974 and 2014! I ummed and aared about including the love songs, but since they come from inside, I finally decided to put some in.

I have chosen to put into print a wide variety of styles, themes and subjects. The works are not in chronological order. To put the writings and pictures in chronological order would give this book too much structure and, for me, destroy some of the innocence.

Only four writings refer to real people, "For VJ", I wrote for my better half in 1980, before we got married. "For JB", written in 1980 about a buddy, who I shall not embarrass by naming him. And also "for CB", a very old buddy who is dying of cancer as I write. The last one is "waiting for you babe", which I wrote for the wedding of Rachel and Craig in August 2014. All other written works are pure figments of my imagination and are not for, or about anyone living or dead.

There is also, no relationship between the poems and the pictures, random!

All benefits and profits from this book will go the Royal Signals benevolent fund. I will not take a penny on the proceeds of this book.

I hope you enjoy reading this as much as I have enjoyed creating it, even if it did take me 40 years!

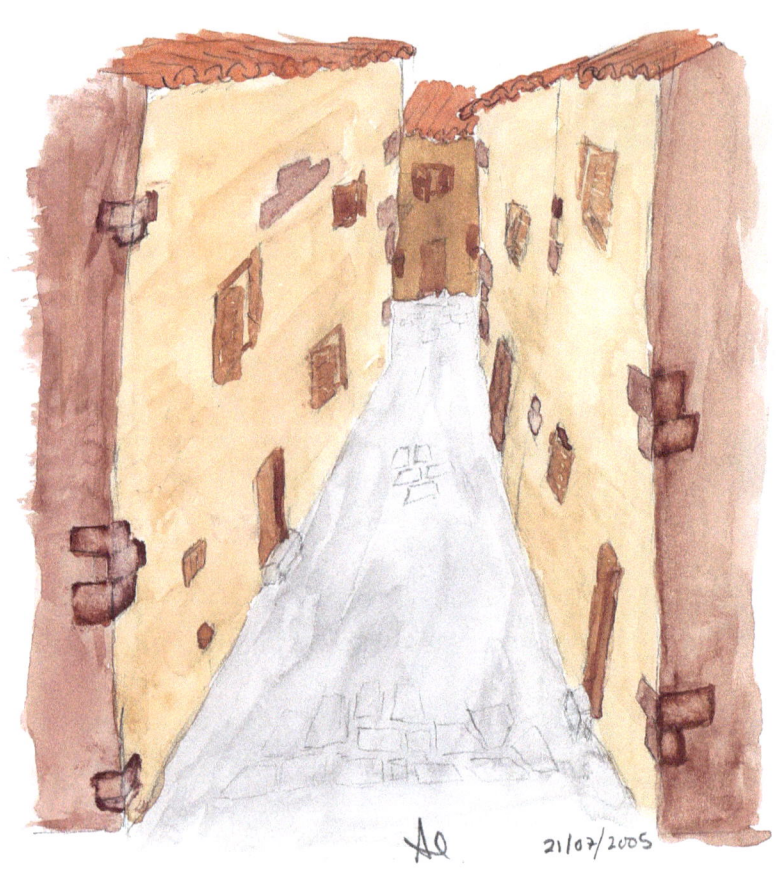

RUE D'AGDE   21/07/2005

A New Dawn

And finally the sun rises
And another day dawns
The stars and moon are fading
And the forest comes to life

And with the light, a new day
And with it comes a new dream
Hope, that the dawn
Is a new dawn of life

The fear and pain must run now
Every ray of sunshine plays its part
The soft breeze moves the air
The sum of the elements change everything

Yes the sun is up
The demons have run
Life abounds
The world can move on!

And as I ponder

And as I ponder what the future may hold
And as I wonder where we will go and how we will get there
Nothing is certain in life; our destiny is in our hands
We will judge, we will manage, we will decide
We will meet, we will smile, and we will bond, again!
We do not know yet, we feel, we hope, we dream
We go up, we go down, we catch up, but we stay in touch
Nay we stay together, through thick and thin we hold out
We will be bad together
Once I am in your arms, I will know
Once you are in my arms, you will know
And only then will we know
Until then we have to survive the ups and downs that are thrown at us

Jagged rock

The sea, all around me is calm, the sun shines and the sky is blue
I am sat quietly on my little jagged rock just above the sea, how did I get here?
The wind picks up and the sea starts to swell.
The wind becomes violent, the waves, strong and vicious
I take my shoes and socks off to keep a better grip on the little rock
I cannot walk away, I cannot fly, only swim away
But swimming in 6 foot waves may not be a good idea
And anyway swim where? Which direction? Where am I?
How did I get here?
I get angry and shout at the wind, it howls through my head
No point, I cannot beat it, I am now cold and wet, I start to shiver
I will sit this out and wait for the sun to dry me out
The night falls, so a few more hours of being cold and wet
I will wait, I am on my own, nothing new, I will sit it out
You will not hurt me wind, deep down inside I cannot be broken, gone too far
No one can hurt me inside again, so make your noise wind, and then just go
How did I get here?
And when the sun comes up I hope she will show me which way to swim

CANAL DU MIDI

24/07/05

Echo

Hello, hello said the echo, echo, echo
Is there anybody there, there, there?
Where have they all gone, these friends of mine?
Who, I once knew long, long ago
The inner truths that we all seek from our own kind
Are like the wind, felt and then let go

Help, help, cried the people, people, people
Will any one come, come, come?
I know you've lost your minds
You, who were once friends of mine,
Look for the truth and maybe you can find
The reality which eludes mankind

Run, run, hailed the leader, leader, leader
Followed by his sheep, sheep, sheep
The automatons, the robots who run their lives
The machine that steals their thoughts
Think for yourself! Go on, take the dive
It's the only way, cos you'll never get taught

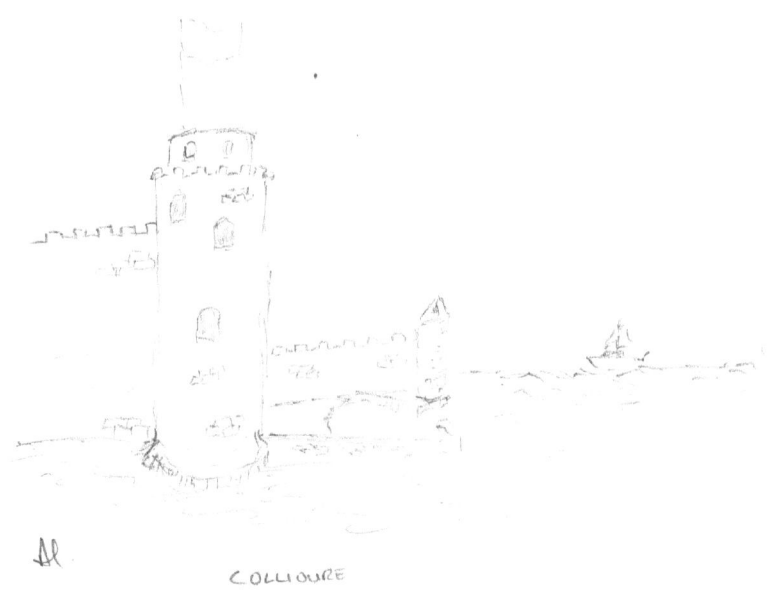

COLLIOURE

The moon

The moon passes through its highest phase
And the tide runs to its highest point
The night is full and people are not at ease
The darkness fills people's minds with fear
In the forest the wolves howl and the bears growl
I walk through this night without fear
I walk through this night, and in the darkness I see a brilliant light
Shining through the forest like a beacon,
I know the light, the same light that guides me during the day, my Sun
And now that same light guides me through the darkness
She does not know she is doing this but she does it all the same
I thought that she was my Sun during the day,
But no she is much more than that, much much more
She is my guiding light which penetrates the void
Light which shines though all weather, any time of day,
She shines for me, from any part of the globe, and I can see!
Her light is my sustenance, my warmth, my life
She is my life and I can walk through any forest as I know she is always with me,
Guiding me, helping me, loving me,
This is a light which is more precious than anything else in the world
I am indeed a very wealthy man then, I have the one and only light!

No Man's land

A   The morning sun unfolds to show the inner paths of light,
         I see a face behind a window beckoning me to come.

B   To lands of mystery and time, of sorrow and of joy,
         And fear unknown to chill the hearts of every mortal man.

1   So come with me my darling to the lands of mystery,
To see what we will find there, beneath the blackened sea.

2   To the lands of time where nothing's found beneath the ageless sea,
Where winds and waves blend noisily in endless harmony.

Chorus A, B

3   So please explore the of sorrow, find out what exists,
All we find are tears and cries and swiftly swirling mists.

4   So come then to a land of joy with happiness and glee,
The safest place that we have found for peaceful sanctuary.

C   The morning sun folds up to cease the inner paths of light
         I see a face behind a window telling me to go.

Liberty

Freedom!! That all-consuming goal, above doubt or criticism
Desired as moths desire the candle
Or immigrants the distant continent
Waiting to parch them in its deserts
Or drive to madness in its bitter winters

Freedom!! That land with rouges at every corner
A place cozen with promises and lies
The plucky sheep who judged it time to sack the shepherd
The fly, to fight in the spiders' web
Something that man will only find in the quiet of death

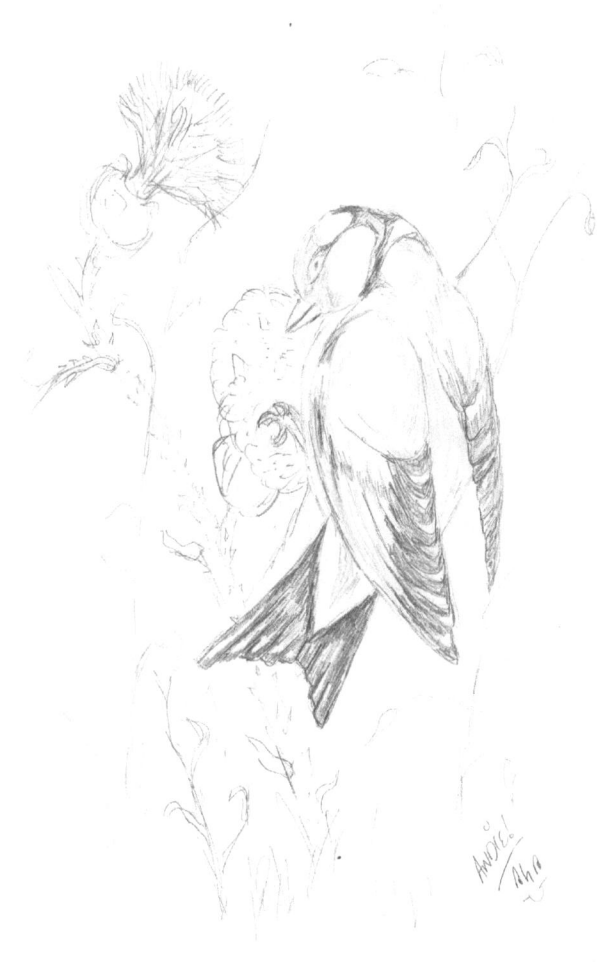

Choice

And if I could choose where I would be tomorrow,
And if I could choose the color of the sky tomorrow
And if I could choose how I would feel tomorrow
And if I could choose who I would be with tomorrow
And if I could choose what I would be doing tomorrow

Then, tomorrow,
I would choose to be at sea, under a deep blue sky, happy, with you and holding your hand

PINK FLAMINGO

Dawn breaks

The sun just starts to seep through the cracks in the shutters
The world starts to come alive and my friend,
Is still asleep beside me, her heart beating so quietly and so slowly,
Her face radiates a warm and loving glow, she smiles in her sleep, I smile
We collided, in our heads and in our hearts, and after the collision came the fusion
Two entities wrapped up in the same point in time space, neither trying to leave
Two hearts beating in time, two minds singing in line
The sun is up and she awakens, the birds start to sing,
And I am happy just to enjoy the moment, another moment of collision as we kiss

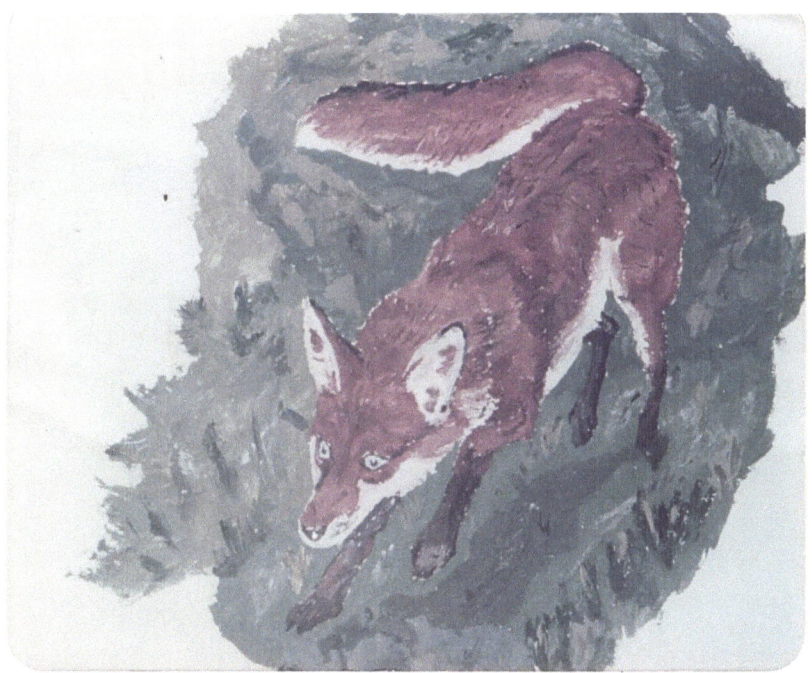

For J B

His pint in his hand, he was himself
A mind untouched, free, alone and wild
The social crowd, they are distant now!
There! Amongst it all a mind that will not hide
He stands alone, yet with them all
Remote, but still the sheepish fool

Cricket he watched and wrote his song
Another mind that I have found
Who, when the leading bell rings loud
Will not turn and follow the crowd
He will stand and sing his song
Along with those who own their minds!

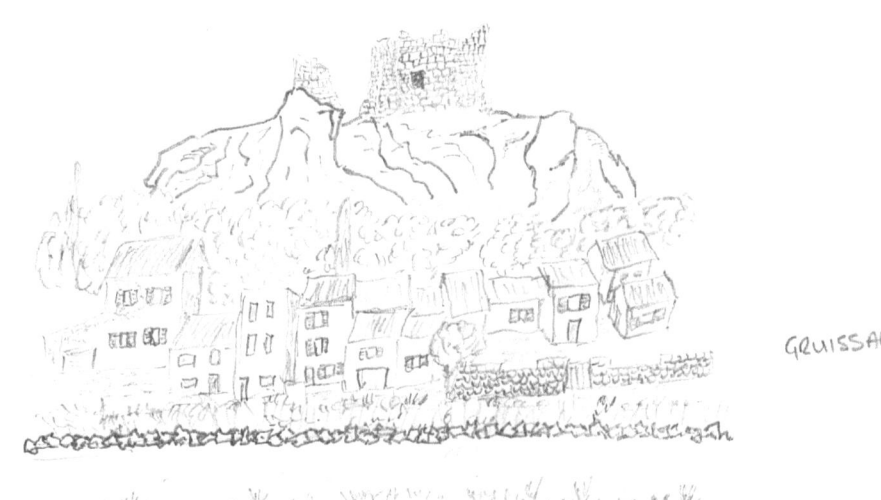

GRUISSAN

For CB

If I were to wish upon a star, which star would I choose?
If I were to choose a star, I would be wishing for it to be the best!
If I were to hope for good to come
How much good would it be, to be hopeful?
And when I dream a dream of desire or wanting
Then my wanting of something shatters the dream
I just wish for him to be at ease

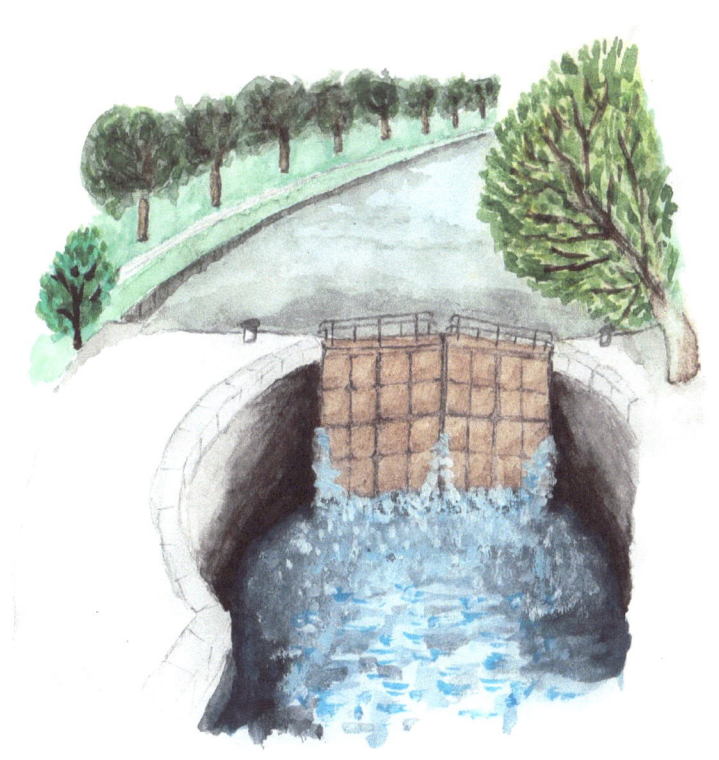

ECLUSE, CANAL DU MIDI
30/07

For VJ

1.   If I give you the words will you write me some notes
And together we'll give them a song
Like the love that we know
Our song it will grow
And we'll show just what we can do
C

2.   Now you know what I mean and see how I feel
My words they must tell you, I know
Your love that's for me
It's plain I can see
It's something we have and can feel
C

3.   Is this what they mean
This thing that we have, only just found
The words of our song
That will lead us along
So that now we can sing it out loud

      C I write about love and sing about love
         And it's easy for others to see
         That I'm in tune with my love
         Because I have found my love

What is a friend?

Many have defined what a friend is, this is my effort

When the wind blows cold on my face I turn to a friend
When my emotions are boiling I turn to a friend
When the forest becomes dark, I turn to a friend
When there is no more light in my life, I turn to a friend
When my heart is burning with loss, I turn to a friend
When the storm rages around me, I turn to a friend
When I am lost and cannot find my way, I turn to a friend
When the moon shines no more and the wolf howls no more, I turn to a friend
When the heat burns my soul, I turn to a friend
And I too stand to help my friends
For that is what we do

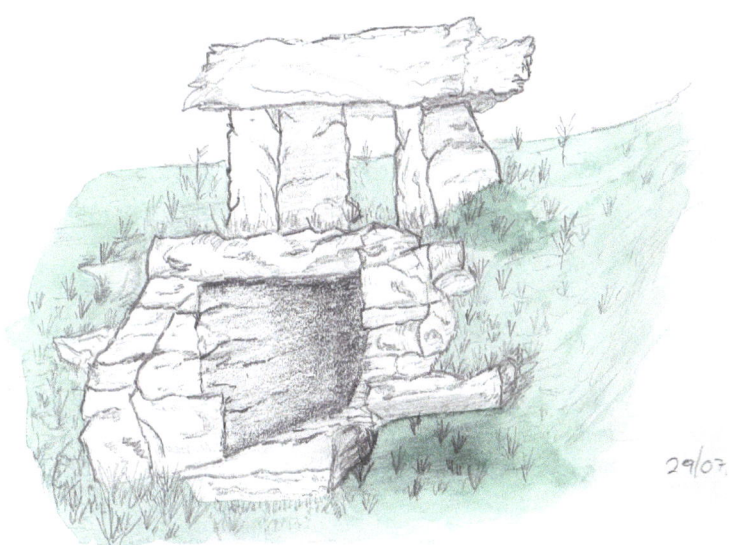

Frightened people

Listen all you frightened people
Standing and staring or just,
Wondering and waiting
It's not such a great achievement
For humanity it's really quite feeble!
In the eyes of the warlords, it's their ultimate toy
This magic mushroom maker, always well placed
Oh it's just great if you wanna destroy
What the hell, yea cos that's all we'll see!
While our leaders battle with their political plight
They all want the mushroom maker for a decisive fight
It's nothing so great and any way we'll never get the ban
It's just another degradation in the life history of man

Hi Babe

Hi Babe, will you go out with me tonight?
I've seen you walking here a dozen times and
Never dared to take the flight!
You walk through my dreams as an angel on fire
I never dared to ask you out, you have always been beyond my reach,
But now you are here, looking at me, within my reach,
Hey Babe will you go out with me tonight,
I look at you and see the light,
I want you and only you, your lips, your hair, your face,
Will you go out with me tonight? Babe?

Goodnight

You are on my mind and will be in my dreams
You will stay under my skin and in my heart
You are beside me in spirit and beside me in will
You help me when I am down
You feed me when I need nourishment
You guide me when I am unsure
You are my guiding light
You are my past, present and my future
I have loved you, I love you and I will love you
Thank you

Just a thought :-)

Happy people

Come and meet some people
Wonderful happy people
No chains, no lies, no plastic, no shit
They think they are free!
Man they are really it
The so called free folk who are just like pencils
Every time you drop them, they crack inside
So help them, even if it against their wills
Cos deep down, there's no place to hide

Heart and Mind

What do I do, when I think I know which way I should go?
My brain has told me to be careful, but my heart has decided
And when my heart has decided, do I know?
So then, when my heart is in control, my intellect has to follow?
But my intellect is sure and my heart is even surer
The battle of wills, who is right in my being
Me, I, Id, has to make a decision, my heart or my intellect?
Difficult, I am in love and need to realise that reality
My intellect will have to take the back seat, whilst my heart explores
And explores and explores…………
The balance, of heart and mind must be maintained
I have that balance, managed and in control
My heart is right... The love I give and receive is undeniable
That love is untouchable, immune to all other influences,
I respect my mind and listen to it, but now, my heart knows where I should go
I follow my heart, I know I am right.

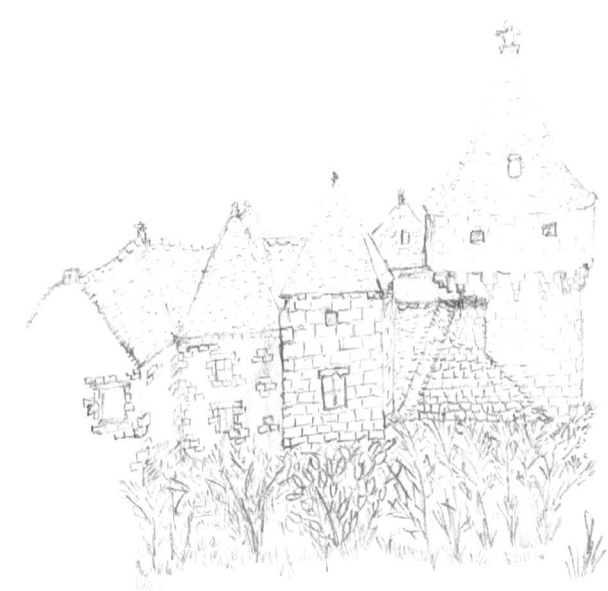

MAISON EN DORDOGNE 03/08/06.

I Care

How can I say that I care??
We can walk and talk in the light of day
All our words and thoughts kept hidden
In our guarded secretive way
And darkness comes
A hint, a sign, then a word in the night
We speak our minds while the walls are down
We must stop now as the dawn brings its light

The day is here and the walls are up
The day is here and I think, think, think

What mark will I leave behind?
How will she ever know I've been here?
What sign will tell her in the future that I existed?
Shall I carve it in the door??

"I am here today…… I exist!"

I believe the deepest impression is made
In those moments when I can say…

I care!

Dream

And as you sleep I dream,
I dream of you
I dream of us
I dream of the future
I dream of our strength together
I dream of a collision, a collision which will create bonds so strong,
nothing will come between us
I dream of two glasses of Rosé, under a summer sun
I dream of preparing food for you
I dream of looking after you
I dream of carrying your bags for you
I dream, I dream and I wait for it to come true

Life

Life, the challenge, the illusion, the enigma
We live it, love it, use it and abuse it
When was the last time you sat down to reflect
Reflect upon your life and the impact you have had on others

Life, to contemplate the very simplest principle of existence
I am here, I do exist, I live, for now
And what then? Have you thought about that?
When now is over and life is ended

We have seen the twilight of others' lives,
We have lived the sorrow of loss
We have felt the pain, the fear, the emotions
And then do you finally fear for yourself?

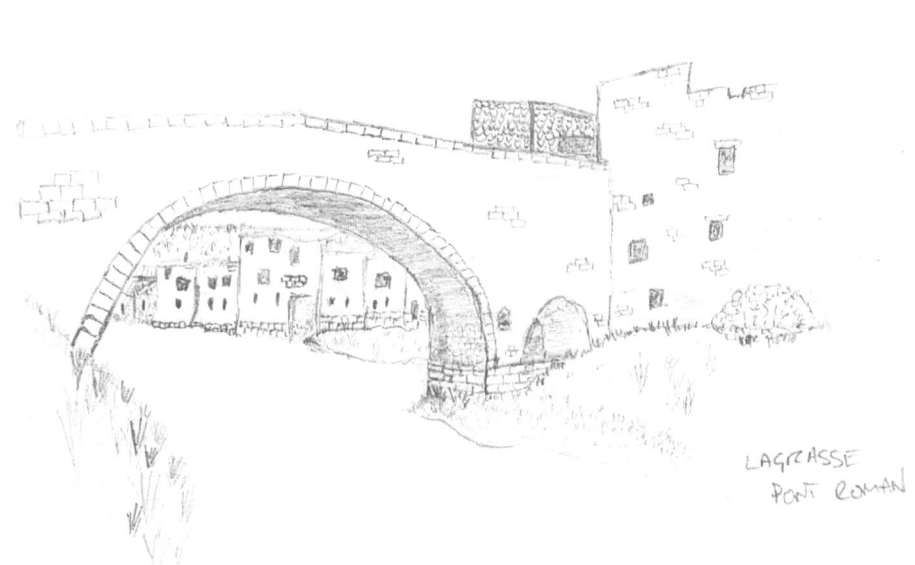

LAGRASSE
PONT ROMAN

My mind is clear

My mind is clear, my heart is firm
It matters not what I want or desire, destiny will decide
My future is not in my hands… Can I influence the future??
It would be very brave to say that I could, but I am brave!
I have a heart next to me, a mind that shines out of the void
A voice that I can hear and understand.
A friend, a hope, peace, and I can see again,
I shall be brave because I have the help and friendship to go there
Destiny? Can I choose or do I decide what I want and then go there?
I will go there!!!!

One life

One life, once chance, one love
The past is behind, only the future can count now
Do we hold to destiny and mould that future, or do we crouch and hide?
There is no alter world, no alternative vision, only the reality that binds us together
Where then??? How to fly, how to swim, how to run?
I will not be tied down to someone else's idea of reality
We feel, we see, we hear, we think, we know!

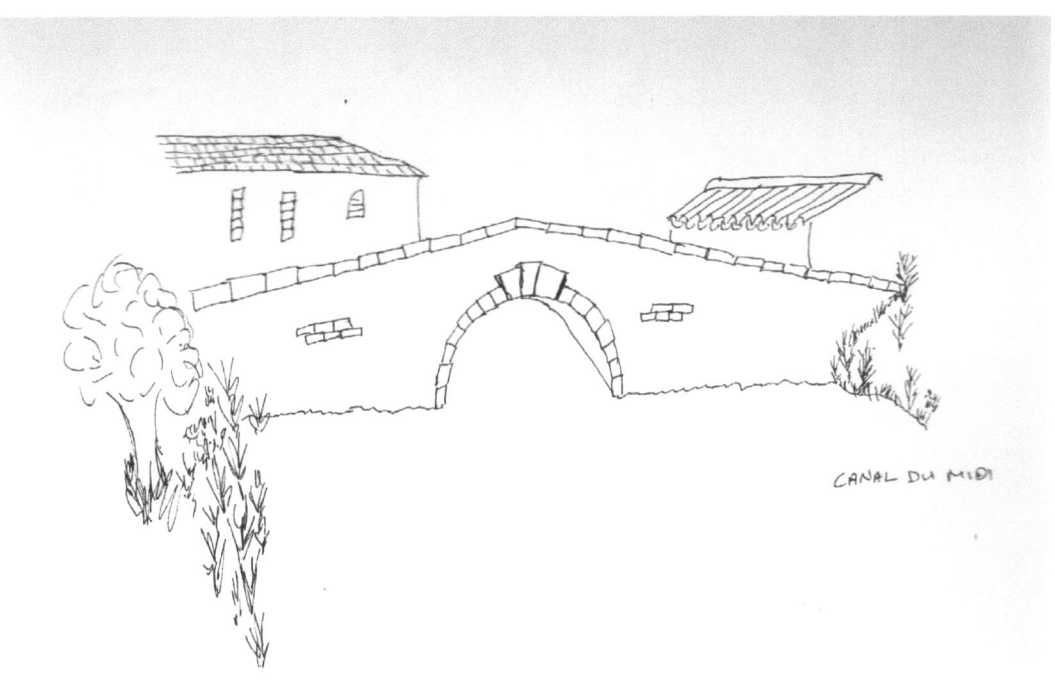

CANAL DU MIDI

Philosophy??

One time
One life
One love
And our experience of reality
Our happiness in the knowledge of that reality

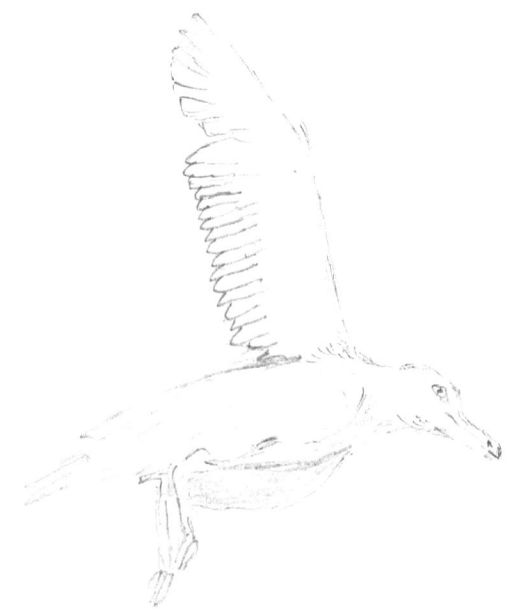

Just wait

Please just wait, a little bit longer
Please just stay a little while more
Please just say that you want me beside you
And then say that you'll stay with me
I will sing you to sleep while I stroke your hair
Listen to your slow soft breathing while you sleep
And then when we meet, I will listen to your slow soft breathing and stroke your hair
And then when we meet, we will know
Please just wait a little bit longer
And expect just a little bit more!

Puppet People

The frauds, the fakers
The merchants, the salesmen
All liars and thieves
Nowhere to run
Nowhere to hide
Around every corner,
The man in a plastic bag
Is waiting for you
The plastic flowers
The Perspex windows
Are just like everyone else we meet
Unreal, false, hidden behind,
Their false fronts and old school ties.

Running

You can run but you can't hide
I can hunt but I won't find
You can think and then be scared
I can watch and then be scared
You can retreat and then say nothing
I can advance and hear nothing
You could talk, if you had the courage
I could listen, if I had no fear
You have run before
I have chased before
You have love, use it well
I have love, which I yield to you
You are running now, with your fear
I am chasing now, trying to get near
You hurt, you are in pain, you cry
I do not understand, I cry
You have a destiny
I have a destiny
Decide, walk the path and talk

Spiral

As I disappear into the winding spiral and descend
The coiled snake raises its head and stares at me
I am confused and cannot see
The spiral goes on down and down, deeper and deeper
The snake is following; I can feel its cold breath on my back
I search with my eyes, reach out with my hands, brake with my feet
Alas, to no avail, I cannot delay or stop the decent
I have been here before, but there was no snake last time
I fight for breath and my stomach tightens
Time to relax and enjoy the ride…. They have no idea…..
It stops, no more spiral decent, just a confused snake in front of me
I have no fear, the still is absolute and the silence is deafening
Relax and enjoy the peace…. Inner calm is the only way out
Faith in one's self and confidence in the ability to climb back out of the pit
It is so cold and it is dark, I have no fear
I close my eyes and think and think and think and there
A small glimmer of light…. It will lead me out
I need to rest, but later, first what I do best, climb………
Sunlight, an ocean, hope……

The mess

The world is a mess, is there no more respect for this cocoon, which has nurtured our species?
What have we done? Why is two thirds of the planet dying of hunger?
Where have the resources gone? The planet is in pain and no one can see it,
Except the few who still have the energy. What can we do, against such overwhelming odds?
The only possible courses of action are all radical! Society would never accept us.
But do we have any choice? I would rather be an outcast than do nothing and see her die.
And you? The other lights in the dark void, what do you say?
Because each on his own has little impact, together the light can truly shine!

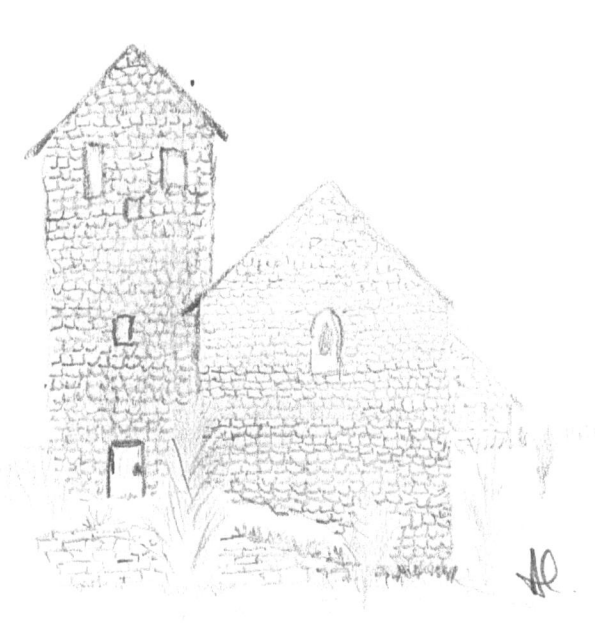

MAISON CAUSSCNARDE

Time

Time, the all-consuming ever present determinant of our lives
And when can we choose what we want to do?
Time, inexorable, waits for no one, Do we wait or do we choose now?
Yesterday, today or tomorrow, when is the right time to choose?
Time, over which we have no power, nor influence
Then choose, make your choice, as the time may never be right!
Time, will wear you down and eventually leave you behind
I have chosen to choose when I want to choose
Time, and I no longer watch the clock, it watches me
Decision taken, time?? you can wait!

To be Aware

All the ears then listen and never hear
All the mouths that open and never speak
All eyes that look and never see
All the noses that are wet and never smell
All the legs that walk and never move
All the brains that think and never solve
All the minds that struggle and never break out
All the poor poor people who have wasted their existence
All around me a black void of empty heads
All this and yet there are still a few sanctuaries in this void
All too few are the small points of light
All this void, yet these few lights are bright enough to warm my mind
Thank you lights! That beam from minds that think and care,
For you have saved me from the void and now, I too, am aware.

Turn to a friend

In times of stress and difficulty I turn to a friend
When my emotions are boiling I turn to a friend
When I am crying and hurting I turn to a friend
When I am lost and lonely I turn to a friend
When I am down and out I turn to a friend

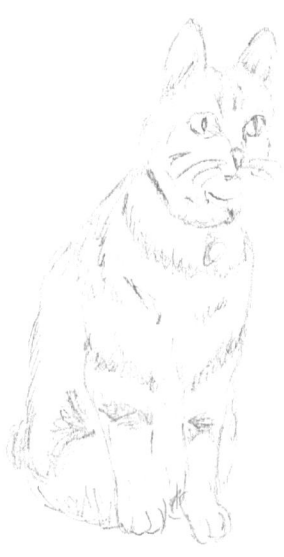

9/10/05   MIPSY

Waiting for you babe

For Rach and Craig 30/08/2014

All of this time, all of these years,
I was waiting for you babe, just waiting for you
We've run the streets, danced the night and seen the light
Again the sun comes up, we are out and still alight
Seen it in Rio, done it in LA, danced it all just right

I was Waiting for you babe, just waiting for you
You came in and stayed, laughed and lived
Went out and left, laughed and lived
And now I know, I'll be there too

I was waiting for you babe, just waiting for you
We cried and screamed, smiled and knew
Lived what is only there for the few
Time goes by and we found what is true

I was Waiting for you babe, just waiting for you
Here you are now pretty one
Really glad you have not gone
No waiting now, almost done

I was Waiting for you babe, just waiting for you
The dance is still alive, the soul still there
You can come and play the poems in the air
I waited, you came and now we share

I was Waiting for you babe, just waiting for you
Open the door, come in and sing
It's all in here and all in a din
It was worth the wait, thank you babe!

Water and life

Look at water;
I sit beside the stream, I watch the water bubble, jump and flow
I sit beside the river, I watch the water moving slowly along its preordained path
I sit on the estuary, I watch the water flow into the sea, majestic, dominant, knowing where it
wants to go
I sit beside the sea, I watch the water being moved by the moon, the life within
I sit beside the ocean, I watch the water, the waves, the ferocity, the power

Then look at life;
The stream, an infant learning to walk
The river, an adolescent learning how to be a member of society
An estuary, a young adult learning how to control his / her life
A Sea, A middle age adult who has learnt how to try and control destiny
An Ocean, A grown up, who knows how to control destiny

Then Life and Love;
The stream, love my mum
The river, trying to love other young ones like myself
The estuary, first real love, get married
A Sea, decisions about what love actually is and where it should go
An Ocean, when we finally work out where we want to go and what love really is.

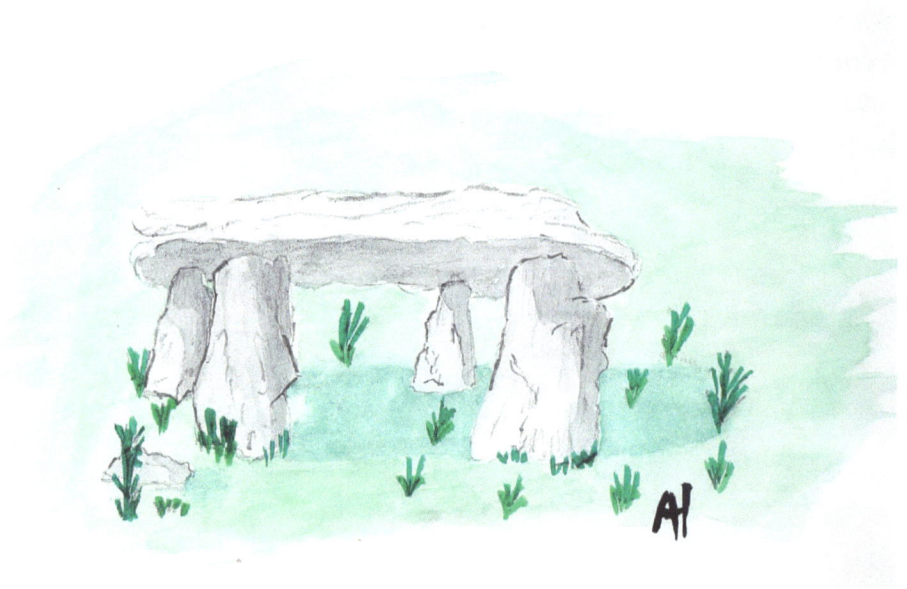

Write a song

Write the lines to a song
Fill the song with the lines of life
And with each line another beat of the heart
As the heart beats the song comes to life
The lines of this song are, yours, mine everybody's
Now there is life to the song
The lines of the song are singing on their own

Write the lines to a song
A song that will come to life
A song that touches all but few will realize
I have written these lines and see the truth
I am writing lines to the song of life
The song is life, life is the song
Live it, sing it, be in it, the music is in my heart

Write the lines to a song
As new lines appear, I see older lines disappearing
I write and I write but the song keeps changing
I write more lines but they are not for me
So I flow with the song, the song of life
The lines are like waves
These are the lines to my song, as I live it

You are

You, are the smile on my face,
You, are the beat of my heart
You, are the butterfly in my stomach
You, are the explosion in my head
You, are the fire in my soul
You, are the Tiger in my jungle
You, are the stars in my sky
You, are the heat of my emotions
You, are the light in my eyes
You, are the Sun in my day
You, are, are, are, are, are, are………. my love!

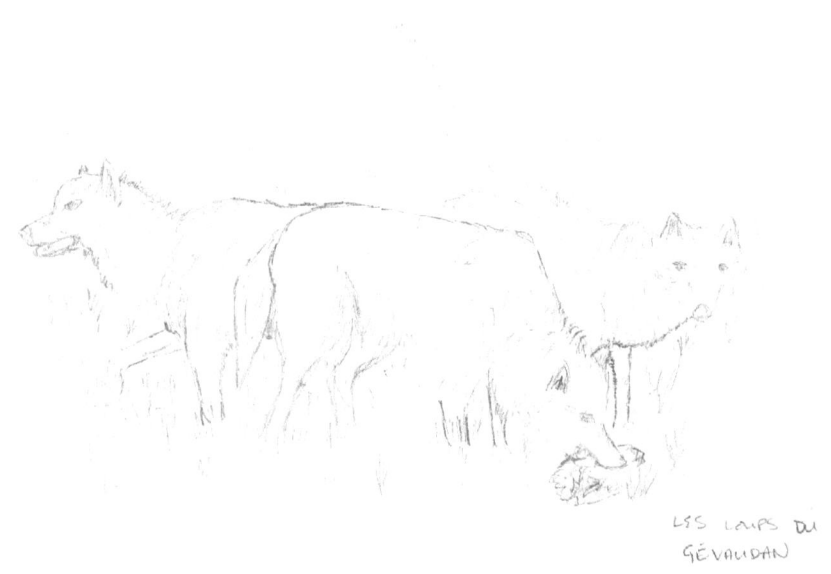

LES LOUPS DU
GÉVAUDAN

www.ingramcontent.com/pod-product-compliance
Lightning Source LLC
Chambersburg PA
CBHW050402180526
45159CB00005B/2115